Bittersweet

Wanda Deglane

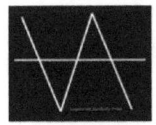

Bittersweet ©2019 by **Wanda Deglane**. Published in the United States by Vegetarian Alcoholic Press. Not one part of this work may be reproduced without expressed written consent from the author. For more information, please contact vegalpress@gmail.com

Cover Art by **Elly Hazard**

Contents

fairy's wings / sweet things	5
frizzy	7
Ode to My Nose	8
ingrained & intertwined	9
Slowly Becoming	11
Training Bras	12
Delicately Misshapen	13
Girl Scout Camp, 2011	14
Overflow	15
Our Skin Has So Much to Say	18
"A Group of Men is Called a Threat"	19
Ode to My First Boyfriend	20
Slut	21
Metamorphosis	22
these hips, this hunger	24
Ladylike	25
Jailbait	26
girls!	27
I thank God you are not my daughter,	28
Ode to the Woman Who Tried to Destroy Me	29
Red-Lipped	30
Serenade	31
Reemergence	32
A Recipe to Create Me	33
Giantess	34
Acknowledgments	

fairy's wings / sweet things

it is a little known fact that
girls can do anything- those
tiny fingers thread life into
november's shy cold.

I'm making shreds of shimmery
lace into makeshift fairy wings.
baby wheelchairs for dolls
when my dog rips their legs off.

I'm stirring weigela petals
into sugar water as a soup for
honey bees. holding the bowl
above my head in the yard,

yelling *come and get it*. I lean in
close to the plants growing
unruly out of sidewalk cracks,
listen to their soft secrets.

and I'm chasing down turquoise-
winged dragonflies before my
lungs know the rasp of terror.
the sun is bleeding indigo

in its wake and somewhere,
my mother is calling my name.
but there is a man emerging
from behind the trees. in the dark,

he is only two wild-gleaming
eyes. he says, *well hello there.*
aren't you a sweet little thing.
my mother's voice tiptoes further

away and his weathered hand traces
my curly hair. *you're like a lil
porcelain doll.* his fingers move
to my cheek and for the first time,

my hands go cold and trembling.
the plants are hushed silent.
for the first time, I can't do anything.
porcelain doll, he says, trancelike.

sweet thing.

frizzy

frizzy hair like muddled daydream,
    like a bass guitar strumming soft   in another room.
frizzy like thunderstorms perpetually pursuing
    my brain.   frizzy like vines twisting
in mother nature's sweetest intimacy, like lightning shock
    in monsoon-battered september.
frizzy like the hairs on my head building cities
    all on their own,   like tangled cumulonimbus and
    whipping knives,
like chocolate waterfalls   and misty rainbows rising
honeyed from the spume.
    frizzy like fingers   getting caught on my skull.
    like bubblegum nightmares.
    like girls in my class
    leaving combs in my desk, snickering,
it looks like you need them.   frizzy like a
    white-hot vengeance,
    like the most tender ferocity.   frizzy hair like
    hundreds of dollars spent on
    a mess of mousses and sprays and creams,
smoke spiraling from
    dark brown strands,   hair fried static-straight
    and suffocating.
frizzy hair   like the most fundamental,
    most inherent part of me.   the endless curls
and waves and tangles that continue growing out of me
    undeterred,   unflinching.

Ode to My Nose

you're too big for this world.
I'm sorry, I didn't make the rules,
nor will I ever read this rulebook that
explicitly states how large a nose can
be while remaining within the narrow,
intangible confines of *pretty*. rounded
wide tip, and crooked from the moment
a soccer ball came hurling at my face,
just seconds after I decided I might be
good at sports after all (I wasn't). I try
to pretend you're not constantly in my
line of vision, like if I can't see you then
maybe you won't be the first thing others
see either. huge and hooked. nostrils wide
as twin suns. every time I cry catching sight
of you in my reflection, every time prim-
nosed girls snicker at you— *nobody wants
a kiss from a beaked girl,* and various slurs of
ethnicities I do not belong to— I place a
dollar in a jar I hide underneath my bed,
labeled *my greatest wish*. giddy for the day I can
finally cut you in pieces, emerge scarred and
bruised but finally, *finally* beautiful. and I'm sorry.
I'll always be sorry. maybe it's not you, it's me.
maybe it's everyone. maybe it's you and me
together, ill-fated to come just shy of everything.

ingrained & intertwined

i.
the first time you feel ugly, your head barely reaches over the sink of your childhood bathroom. your mother is brushing your hair, one fistful clenched in a cold steel grip, the other hand tearing away at your tangles so violently it brings tears to your eyes. she's growling at your hair like an animal, screaming at its inability to lie flat and smooth and shiny. in your shadows you see the curls and cowlicks shooting out of your head like vines, and you want an axe, a drought, a lawnmower, anything. your friend gives you beautiful barrettes and scrunchies for Christmas and your mother laughs dryly. *don't be fooled. it's because your hair is ugly.* you shake your head but the word gets caught in the knots.

ii.
ugly stinks of blackened juice of rotten fruit, of fish left to die on blistering boardwalk, of the concoctions of milk and apple juice and mustard the boys make to fling at each other during lunchtime. ugly smells putrid, and the more you grow, the more you believe you must reek of it. it sits beside you in silence, never shouted at you directly, but you were much too observant to miss its little hints. all the days spent trying to sell girl scout cookies, and the hordes of adults walking through you like a tiny phantom. all the girls shifting instinctively away from you like deep down you must be roach. all the teachers who intertwined your being *not cute* with *not smart* or *talented* or *much of anything, really*. you become more accustomed to being no one's favorite, to floating mute and undetected through your own world. you sit so long in this *ugly*, it starts to grow fruit around you.

iii.
and with ugly comes its lonely sister, dancing wild in your lungs, scooping out your innards like you're a big-nosed, frizzy-haired pumpkin. your brain forms friends out of tree branches and ladybugs and patterns on a wooden table. you paint the sweetest words on their imaginary mouths, picture their eyes staring back at you with the most intoxicating softness.

iv.
one day you sneak into your mother's room and drown your face in her makeup, try to kill the imperfections you can't stand with endless powders and creams and brightly colored things. you make your face into a rainbow, an artwork, burying

tears and laughter and long-forgotten years of dancing carefree on the sun. unveil yourself in the mirror and find--
        a splattered, claw-torn canvas,   mismatched fabrics sewn haphazardly together,
        a dead house painted over garrish red,   a cockroach suffocated in lipstick.
you hide wailing under shreds of your own self-worth, let the ugly open its starving, lying lips and take another taste of you.

Slowly Becoming

this is how you learn to live in a woman's
body / it starts slow, like winter dawn /
more hair here, more hip there / so many
more questions / but discomfort sits heavy
on your tongue / your hair loses its curls /
your face its baby cheeks / your body is
becoming a wasp / more sting in this skin /
your body is becoming a leap year / a spiraling
mountain interstate / a sweet tooth / a
childhood house caught on fire / and what
do you do / with a body you merely stumbled
into? / a body that feels more park bench
than home? / this is how they teach you /
to live in a woman's body in catholic school /
baggies full of menstrual pads / and travel-sized
teen spirit / scientific diagrams of / what lives
between your legs / no *labia* / no *clitoris* / just
a sterile voice saying / *this is the uterus* / *these are
the tubes* / over the sound of / 11 year old boys
snickering / glancing at your shorts / then back up
at you / like they can see through your flesh / your
bones /your fragile girlhood / this is how you
learn to live in a woman's body / to define your
worth by / how many men you attract /
and how much they can put inside you.

Training Bras

we hardly remember the day our bodies start
changing. the slippery moment of bones and
organs shifting and expanding from tiny slender girl
to this soft, fleshy thing, all hips and thighs and bellies.
our hands swell to saucers and our feet follow suit like
the most uncoordinated dance. bodies developing more
and more unfamiliar, stumbling on its own becoming.
look at this velvet skin. look at these unproportional
parts, becoming flickering porch light and squashed
evening sun and everything that glitters. we change for
PE in shivering silence, avert our eyes from blossoming
c-cups and chests flat as tree trunks. glance down our
own shirts at the barely-budding twin lemons nestled
there. we learn to undress quickly in supply closets and
underneath desks, taking turns away from sneaking boy
eyes in the windows. if we aren't careful, if we don't warily
watch each move our bodies make, we'll feel that familiar
snapping of straps, taunting voices saying, *nice training bra.
mind showing me a little more?* there are girls among us whose
bodies are already rose gardens- bras already filled by fifth
grade and curves flowing in and out like drunken roads.
we watch them with jealousy and pity interweaving in our
chests- the way all the boys gawk hungrily. the way they
sometimes reach out and touch like those bodies are public
playgrounds. we whisper to each other of what to do when
men start to look too long, when they grope and sneer.
what to do with hair underneath our arms and blood spilling
sweet on cotton panties. we still cry into each other's chests.
we still hold hands in the dark.

Delicately Misshapen

my body is ruined city / is a dump truck lit on fire
and swerving wildly / the odd shape my skin makes / like
it forgot halfway through just what it wanted to be / flat,
misshapen butt / and breasts like baby yellowjacket stings /
not twins but distant cousins that avoid each other's
uncomfortable gaze / I am watching lithe girls move
delicate as if floating / like clouds catching rain in the silk
of their hair / I hate every one of my movements I watch
closely in the mirror / awkward, hesitant, stumbling / sky
taking bites out of my body with each step / I dress not like
a girl flowering with life / but as if I'm already concealing
a cadaver in its body bag / every eye must be following me /
must be thinking / *look at that dumpy, drooping, disfigured girl /
look at that body, lopsided and bloated and too immense to avoid* / I am
sucking in my breath so hard / my ribs threaten to bend in half /
I am pinching off the pale, flabby flesh covering my belly / that
turns bright red and then purple but never quite melts away /
I am feeding my organs more loathing than sustenance / how
they beg beneath my fingertips / while I weep at the way I only
grow larger and more lumpy / one day I will eat this body like a
bland, too-chewy hors d'oeuvre / gnaw away at the fat growing
uncertain in every wrong spot / I give rough hands secure places
to hold onto / I am making myself something worth looking at /
something beautiful to the touch.

Girl Scout Camp, 2011

on the drive into the trees, we were
the catastrophe, but never the story
behind it. they came in through the
window one night, sweetened by pitch
blackness. slender and sixteen and
beautiful, they snickered at us in our
long pajamas, our creaky bunk beds.
who are you, we said. we were barely twelve.
they were high school girls, bored and
barbaric all at once. we gathered 'round
them like disciples and they told us how
beer tastes like young adulthood feels—
a plunging, a thrusting, a sickening, a
dying all in your mouth. *how many of you
girls know how to give a man a blow job?*
some of us nodded, but none of us
really knew. they passed around a tube
of toothpaste, showed us that when
your throat is heaving and you're feeling
a little less human, that means you're
doing it right. they showed us how to
shake our asses, how to taste the inside
of another girl's mouth, how to be a
spectacle and a three-course meal and a
playful, gaping hole. and when we could
no longer stomach the unease, the shame,
they said, *our prodigies. our little naturals.*
they ducked back out the window
as the sky lit its own belly on fire.

Overflow

i.
the first time my period comes,
it starts in my knees, a tender

shivering ache that travels to my
lower back, to the space between

my blooming hips. the howl that breaks
from my mouth is one of a girl dying,

wounded. I burst into my mother's
bedroom, flowered underwear pulled

down to my thighs, at once both terrified
and brazen. she tells me I'm not dying,

and hands me a pad, its yellow wrapper
crinkling in my whitened grip. no, I'm not

dying, she assures me. I am beginning anew.

ii.
I am in seventh grade, sobbing in the
bathroom stall of a water park. I tell

my mother over the phone, *I wasn't
expecting it today and I don't know what to do.*

how am I supposed to swim now? she says,
I'm sorry, honey, I guess you can't. but when

I say, *I can wear a tampon. they have a machine
here that sells them,* she says, *no no no no no,*

repeatedly, vehemently. I ask her why until
my throat goes hoarse, until she finally says,

only sluts wear tampons. and
no daughter of mine will be a slut.

iii.
spotted panties at age 12 in the line at
krispy kreme, white skirted and mortified,

and again in my seat in the middle
of freshman english class, and yet

again in the backseat of a car at 19
years old. it doesn't stop being new,

nor unpredictable. I'm washing my pants
in the bathroom sink, earning these stains

like little battle scars shoved further
and further into my underwear drawer.

iv.
boys who scoff and say, *god, she's pissed.*
she must be on the rag. boys who

tremble at the slightest scrape,
the miles-away scent of blood, but say,

I've been hit in the balls before. that hurts
way worse than anything you've felt.

I smile thinly, mutely. look back on
all those doubled-over, heat-padded nights.

the clammy pale of my skin as my vision
fizzles, no ibuprofen at hand.

the sway of my body on a toilet bowl stained

scarlet, like lake overflowing with rose petals.

the casual spilling of my flesh, like it's
effortless, like it's painless, like it's not

the most beautifully brutal thing I've ever done.

Our Skin Has So Much to Say

you are 13 years old and made of fresh
cotton- half of you is tied to the sky. the other
half only knows how to fall apart. your friends
are shoving push pins into their hands during
class. they come to school each day wearing more
and more horizontal lines on their arms like
new bracelets. sometimes they start to spell
the beginnings of words. unfinished thoughts.
misplaced mourning. you can't stop your eyes
from searching for scars. you're watching warily
each time your friends come too close to railings.
a callous teacher tells you, *don't worry. if they jump,
all they'll do is break bones.* so you take matters into
your own hands, begging them to stop, to
apologize to their own limbs. they blink at you
like you just don't understand, and maybe you don't.
one night, you dive your fingers into a lit candle
without thinking. you jerk away immediately,
terrified at your own boldness. and tentatively,
you try again, letting flame lick hungrily at your
fingertips, then your wrists, then all the places
grief has touched your body. as the fire slowly dies
out, you lean back into bed, drunk on the smell of
burning flesh and vanilla, tracing your blisters like
new constellations in the dark. you're whispering,
I'm sorry. this isn't personal.

A Group of Men is Called a Threat

1.
cling tight to your mother's hand everywhere you walk. never wander, trail behind. when she insists on keeping you in her sight, you want to sigh, but even still- though your brother, only a year older than you, comes and goes as he pleases, your mother stands at the front door as you cross the street to the neighbor's house. she says, *I need to watch you.* she says, *don't ever get caught alone, especially with a man. god only knows what could happen.*

2.
your coming-of-age present is hot pink pepper spray to fill the spaces your mother no longer can. you clutch it on your walks home after dark like a lifeline, fingers white and ready. the shadows tiptoe closer, breath hot at your neck. every streetlight, every passerby is a sanctuary. your mind is whipping wildly through every story you've heard of girls who never learned how to scream or keep their keys between their fingers like a fear-forged weapon. stand up straight and walk quick, don't look sweet but don't look cocky either. wear headphones, and when a man starts to leer at you and shout, crank up the music to deafening, and walk faster. and when you make it home, lock the door behind you and *exhale.*

3.
your footsteps are silent, your voice irreversibly hushed. this is how you survive, by mastering the art of being utterly *soundless*, of passing by undetected. be dumb. be helpless. laugh sweet and say *thank you*, but don't ever say *no* or *leave me alone*, even when your skin is shrieking. let your tongue grow comfortable only in the guilt-heavy *I'm sorry.*

4.
and yet when every other girl you know tells you the same story of men screaming filth at her in the streets, ripping the clothes from her thrashing body as deafening music drowns out her voice, all you can do is nod. all you can say is, *I know.*

Ode to My First Boyfriend

my favorite piece of you was the one that decided
        I was worth loving. I looked at you and saw *tower*,
            saw oversized raincoat, saw underground bunker-

      never quite comfortable enough to find a home
in you, only a safe spot to hide from my own
        blustering self-hatred. there were roses and

        chocolates, teddy bears and too-tender birthday
    cards, your arms snaked around me like your
possession, and my tangible tension, my mouth

      never knowing how exactly to say no. could you
        blame me? a girl is a girl is a farm animal- all my
worth dependent on the meat I could offer, and

how many boys thought me good enough to own.
           the first time you held my hand was a hunt: your hand
              a pouncing predator, mine the panicked fleeting bird.

      ensnared and uncomfortable, semi-cherished but
put me out of my misery. my least favorite piece
      of me was the one that decided I owed you my

        self in exchange for your affection- because who
    else could love something so widely undesired?
I wish I could tell you there was a piece of me

        that wanted badly enough to believe this was true,
           everlasting, but my hands found their desperately-
    craved freedom, and your gifts found a new grave

at the bottom of my trash can.

Slut

i.

when my teacher calls me a slut, I am thirteen and a boy has just hugged me. she says nothing to the boy. I am wearing what all other girls at my catholic school wear: red polo shirt, plaid skirt. the boy takes off running while I stand there, too stunned to cry and too wounded to move, like an icy shard from the heavens has just pierced me to the floor.

ii.

when my teacher calls me a slut, I believe her. my lips have never met anything but my mother's cheek, but in my teacher's eyes I am lying naked, legs spread and sultry. she says *slut* but I hear *filthy*, I hear *worthless*. every time I pass my reflection, I see the *whore* she sees, and my heart crawls farther into my ribcage to hide. my mother asks that evening how my day went, but I'm too ashamed to tell her the new word I learned.

iii.

when my teacher calls me a slut, it is loud. it is noticeable. it is as palpable in the air as choking, sticky moisture. it is head-turning, a dog whistle for every other thirteen-year-old within a mile. she says, *I can't trust you on your own*, and, *who's next on your list?* and, *look at all these boys you ruin.* she speaks of girls who fall pregnant at fifteen, who waste their futures pleasing men on their backs, and the whole time she's looking at me. and so is everyone else.

iv.

when my teacher calls me a slut, it is forever. it is carved in my skin by a rusted knife. I scrub and scrape away at the words but they only inch deeper. when she calls me a slut, it follows me, lingering in every strand of my hair, in the breath streaming from my mouth, in the sour-slanted looks boys will give me for years to come. it is a giant nametag super-glued to everything I own, everyone I become. I'm punching every mirror that glances twice at me. I'm shaking and shaking and shaking my body but the *slut* won't pry loose.

Metamorphosis

it is 2013 and a boy is telling me
he loves me and I'm 14 so how
could I not believe him? he's loved
five other girls already this year,
but now he loves *me* and that
makes me special, makes me chosen.
he texts me, *you're so pretty. you have
such soft skin,* and my heart has never
known such drunken swelling.

it is 2013 and my first kiss happens
almost by accident. he reaches to
kiss my cheek and I turn too quick
and suddenly we are a tumbled
car wreck of teeth and braces.
he says we need to get better at this
and so we practice— after school and
behind brick walls and at the ends
of dark hallways. I'm imagining
new year's eve and the final scene
of a rom com. I'm becoming the girl
I always dreamed of.

it is 2013 and he unceremoniously
texts, *I wanna fuck you,* and my
stomach drops down to my hips and
I try to tell myself this is what butterflies
must feel like, when it really feels like a
thousand cocoons lit on fire, dropping
to the earth to be trampled underfoot,
like cancelled metamorphosis. he waves
a condom in my face and tells me to
get ready, and everything from my hair to
my toes feels green, innocent, childlike.
this is for me and no one else, I say as I crouch
behind the locked bathroom door, shaving
the holy land between my legs. thick black

curls fall to the trash can as I bloom
baby smooth. I may not yet be woman but
I can pretend.

it is 2013 and he becomes too familiar
with all the bras I own. the cream-colored
ones, the ribboned and polka-dotted
ones I bought just for me. he gropes at
my boobs in the middle of lunch, small,
barely budding things they are, and my
friends glance away uncomfortably. reluctant
organs and dried up oceans. I stare down
at my hot pocket and wonder how someone
can so easily take something that is so *mine*.

it is 2013 and I am learning there are
pieces of me I no longer own. it is 2013
and I am learning to master the art of
being *likeable*- nodding and smiling and
spreading and giving and giving and giving.

these hips, this hunger

what is a skipped meal   or two
      when my skirt falls several inches
   from my hips? what is a couple pounds
or 15   when he cups
       my waist   like a birdcage
and holds my jaw in his hands, saying,
     I love what little
   is left of you.
what is a face   drained of color,   the lacunas
      left behind by my cheeks
melting away,   when my mother finally
      kisses   my knife-arms,
   my ghost-eyes, an echo of
the body   she always wanted?
   my shoulder blades   are bat wings
my blood is skinny blue   yet
       I've never been so in love
           with such sickness.
tonight I lie, back flat to the soil,   and trace
      the summits of the mountains
      my hips have become.
I ignore the starving screams   from
   the valley below.

Ladylike

bend down, not over.

                      I catch my male friends' eyes straying to my rear,
straighten up immediately, face beet-red
and pulsing hot. I receive a text message
later that night, a photo attached.
black lace panties? that's hot.
I throw my phone across the room,
stare at the ceiling as something bitter
and sharp claws its way around my chest.

men don't like a girl with a big mouth.

                      my high school boyfriend tries to tie my tongue
to the back of my throat, but fire knows no
restraints. I keep my mouth restless, screaming.
he keeps his hands ready.

no one cares if you're smart or
kind or funny, as long as you're pretty.
be pretty. it's all that matters in this world.

                      I'm in shoes that pinch my toes blistery-pink,
a dress that squeezes me in all the wrong
places. I burn my hair to anti-frizzy perfection
and wobble to walk straight. a boy catches
sight of me, leans over to his friend to whisper
what he thinks I can't hear: *she's flat as a board.*
I'll give anyone fifty dollars if they can find her ass.
I go home early and rip my reflection
to pieces in my bare hands.

don't say yes. but don't ever say no, either.

                      what is this fine line I'm straddling? the tongue
that once knew no limits now tiptoes sweetly
in my mouth. I train my face to look coy but sultry
for the nudes he demands, but I don't know how to ask
him if he sees me as a human being. in the library,
his hands wander down the front of my blouse. past
the zippers of my shorts. I stare straight ahead, like
I can't watch my own body's defilement.
people are staring. they're saying, *what a slut.*
they're saying, *this is why you need to act like a lady.*

Jailbait

on the bus ride back to phoenix,
rough 18-year-old hands part your
15-year-old knees. he whispers, *I love
when you wear skirts.* which is to say,
he loves easy access. he loves how
easy you are. he nuzzles your cheek
where stubble has already rubbed your
soft skin raw. your eyes wander out
the window, at strip malls and tiny brown
houses flying by like sun-trimmed
memories. you will your mind to
evaporate, your nerve-endings to die.
mouth too big for your mouth, tongue
swallowing the last of your self-esteem.
eyes piercing holes in you from all
directions. his hands are in your hair and
you're thinking of how incomprehensibly
huge they are, of how much you want
to love him, if only to numb this burn
a little. you're wondering what it means
to love in the first place.

girls!

I didn't know I liked girls even though they'd pile up in my dreams with giant soft honey eyes and red lips curling like crescent moons. I didn't know I liked girls because when they'd dance across my mind, they'd be carrying a sign screaming *SINNER* in bright bold letters. what is this heart-soaring, this warming all over? all these years spent sifting through my own immorality, thinking, *do I admire this girl? am I envious? or do I want to dive into the velvet of her skin? do I want to taste the sun in her hair?* one of my best friends sees a gorgeous woman with a pixie-cut and says, *look at that dyke*, that one syllable smashing my organs. I didn't know I liked girls because I couldn't imagine a world where that would be okay. my father watches two women kiss and grimaces in disgust, says to me, *thank god you'll only ever be some man's wife*. all these years wasted sobbing, confessing, stifling my sweet only in fleeting thoughts and shame-splattered dreams. letting boys wander into my body, my mouth, like an unlocked house because maybe one day it would kill the unnatural in me. there are girls living in my heart, and they will never die. they plant apple trees and beg me to have a taste. one day, I'll bring one home, take her coat at the door and lace my fingers through hers. I'll say, *mom, dad, this is my girlfriend*. I'll say, *congratulate me. I'm finally home.*

I thank God you are not my daughter,

say the women walking briskly past me on
the street, the chaperones at my high school
dances, the mothers at my graduation. girl in
the low-cut tops, sin dripping from my skin like
sweat. God only knows girls need correcting,
the women think to themselves, and one like me
would soak up their beatings like air until their
hands became sore. *I thank God you are not my
daughter*, the women sing praises bowing servile
at the foot of their beds. because there must be
something wrong with girls like me, some feral
gene spreading mutant in all my cells that makes
boys look at me and think *prey*, that turns sweet
sons into rapists. The women kiss the heads of
their own daughters, mute and turtlenecked and
heads ducked, and thank God their girls were not
born temptresses. they know what it means to be
the *yes* girl, the ever-smiling wife. *I thank God you
are not my mother*, I tell them. I shirk the blame
from my crimeless shoulders, shed the shame like
ill-fitting burn wounds. I eat their disgust like a
fish hook embedded in my tongue.

Ode to the Woman Who Tried to Destroy Me
after Maitreyi Ray

call me *slut*. call me vomit-colored soul. call me pig
too filthy for slaughter. sit at the back with the other
parents during my high school volleyball games and
call me *vixen*, call me slime-toothed *viper*. point out how
tight my shorts are to the other moms and say, *that's the
little whore*. say it just loud enough for me to hear. call me
gutter rain. call me rot, call me eternal slop. call me bird
corpse licked clean of life. check each one of my teeth like
a horse and call them bloated, drowned children. take those
photos you keep of me and parade them to every son you
find: my 15-year-old body posed naked and trembling. small
breasts and rib cages so heaving and white they scream
surrender. collect my dead skin cells and sell them as ashes.
call me *slut*, call me *temptress*, but do not call me slug. don't
call me gray-skinned or beaten or half-eaten. don't call me
wounded, feeble, tepid cunt. I am growing sure into the
blooms you tried to light on fire. I am draining my blood
clean of your venom. I am claiming this body a whole planet,
a liberation, a fucking force of nature.

Red-Lipped

there comes an autumn when I stop wearing
thick black eyeliner to cover tear-swollen sockets,
replace it instead with painted lips, bright red or
deep crimson to suit my mood. let the sun eat my
hair crushed gold. let these arms become owl wings,
each finger a whole weapon. let this tongue form
giddy ribbons around the word *no*. my reflection is
my own girlfriend, she kisses even my belly fat, even
these dusk-dark circles settling under tired eyes. I wear
these tight shirts and short skirts like they've married
my skin. I swallow more crocodile tears and collarbones
than shame these days, more hips than guilt. the secret
to losing all the names they'd call me is to grow new
flesh, let it harden sweet like candied egg shells. go ahead,
have a poke. I'll sit comfortable in my own pretty skull.
dig inside it and you'll find gape-mouthed sunfish. dig
deeper and you'll find a sea of bats. and even deeper still
are tiny teacup pigs. this fierce, tender thing isn't going
anywhere. I am sweetness and vengeance. I am a molten
lava / honey concoction. I am daisies dancing free of
flames. the secret to being woman isn't painting your lips
red and smiling lovely. it's in giving those lips the keys
to open wide and say *fuck you*.

Serenade

i love you, my skin. soft as raspberries, soft as memories, soft as grayest sun at the birth of a new day, growing thicker every minute. my bruises from all the clumsy bumps and stumbles. the scratches from the eager paws of my dogs. the ever-present scar from the day Michael Jackson died. i love you, my hair. my whipping, frizzy frenzy, dry as the phoenix air. forgive me for the years i resented you, the mornings i'd dip you in flames to make you flat as death. i love you my thighs, with the puckered skin, the sweat that glues you together in summer. it is a privilege to peel you from leather seats everywhere i sit. i love you, my belly, with some hair here and there, paler than the rest of me, and always with that layer of blubber no matter how many miles i sprint. how you cushion my organs so sweetly even on days i refuse to eat. i love you, my nose, so huge and mediterranean. i saved up money my whole life to chop you to pieces and i burst into tears every time someone looked at you differently- my longest, closest friend, who would i be without you? i love you, my too-large feet, my too-wide forehead, my crooked, tiny teeth, my dark purple that's refused to abandon the space beneath my eyes. i love you my skinny legs, my chubby arms, and all the silken plush that is my body: the rounded angles, the hazy lines. every one of my muscles, my bones, my cells, i love you i love you i love you.

Reemergence

today I bleed on everything I own,
wake on top of crimson splotches.
this tiny massacre in my pants. I wash
my underwear with hand soap in the
sink, squeeze scarlet from my fingertips.
today I am bloated beast, that pouch
of organs swelling painful under warm
flesh. today I am bare-faced, soft-
skinned. I burrow under blankets and
sleep well into noon's embrace. I swim
inside myself and find islands dotting
the sun. I am not these blood stains,
nor the bird skulls waiting outside my
front door. I am not a waist-to-hip ratio,
or a dew-kissed flower. I am not face
symmetry or legs pinned back or a
welcome mat spread across my cervix.
I am woman and life-breathing hips
and mouth big enough to hold a moon-
sized fist. I am skin and sweet and sex
and power and love. today I bleed on
everything I own, because everything
I own begs to hold a piece of me.

A Recipe to Create Me

1. take the lone child of bittersweet whalesong and house fires started by christmas lights.
2. fill her insides with tree sap. with paper cranes made out of high school detention slips. with cherry-stained baby teeth and light-blurring headache.
3. where there should be attachment, stuff down rage. and where there should be self-doubt, only more rage.
4. pickle her heart in a jar and fill the spaces in between with teary-eyed fireflies, frozen forever to sing only in light.
5. stuff one lung with tiny marshmallows. toss a lit match in there too. shut it tight and don't mind the smoke.
6. where there should be a golden-lined soul, give her a forest nymph spirit. give her a fear of the ocean and of tall white men. give her fingers like butter knives that fall just a little too crooked.
7. coat her with skin translucent as a dream, stretched thin like elastic. glittery. unbreakable.
8. mold her nose out of Greek goddess marble. steal her eyes from star-pooled lagoons. store her brain in ivy and vanilla ice cream and electric eels.
9. name her december. name her supermoon. name her god.
10. wake her up and tell her what a worthless piece of shit she is. tell her she'll never accomplish anything. watch her stand up at once and prove you wrong.

Giantess

you must know by now:
    to love yourself is to be perpetually   angry,
is to dismantle   everything & anything
        you've ever seen & learned & been
in all your past lives,
    feed those pieces to the manta rays   & watch
them float to heaven.
              & rebuild every limb & every
organ   into hedera-drowned cities, into lakes pulsing sweet
                with honeyed milk.
      to love yourself is to bury old car fires
    in a mouthful of dirt,   hold grief close
like a lover, let her sing   but never stay the night.
    loving yourself is not a becoming,
        but a physical swelling.   you'll say:
look at me, I'm colossal.   *I'm a universe.*
                I'm fucking exquisite.
& everyone you know will have to tip their heads back
    to see your face, glowing & soaring &
        sipping stratosphere,   & they will tremble.
to love yourself is to kiss your past mistakes   with tongue,
      to absorb silver-lined self-compassion
          in every pore.
you may be eating your own tail, but you chew slowly.
      you savor it.

Acknowledgments

Thank you infinitely to the editors of these incredible journals that published the following poems, sometimes in earlier versions:

Little Lion Literary : "frizzy" and "A Recipe to Create Me"

Eunoia Review : "Ingrained & Intertwined," "Red-Lipped," and "Ode to My First Boyfriend"

Neon Mariposa Magazine : "Slowly Becoming"

Rose Quartz Magazine : "Girl Scout Camp, 2011" and "A Group of Men is Called a Threat"

Lux Undergraduate Creative Review : "A Group of Men is Called a Threat"

Selcouth Station : "Overflow" and "Our Skin Has So Much to Say"

Picaroon Poetry : "Slut"

Rag Queen Periodical : "Metamorphosis"

Homology Lit : "These Hips, This Hunger"

Mooky Chick : "Ladylike"

Pulp Poets Press : "Jailbait"

The Fruit Tree Magazine & *Perfectly Normal Zine* : "Girls!"

Kissing Dynamite : "I thank God you are not my daughter"

Sidereal Magazine : "Ode to the Woman Who Tried to Destroy Me"

L'Ephemere Review : "Serenade"

Vamp Cat : "Giantess"

Wanda Deglane is a night-blooming desert flower from Arizona. She is the daughter of Peruvian immigrants and attends Arizona State University. Her poetry has been published or forthcoming from *Rust + Moth, Glass Poetry, Drunk Monkeys, Yes Poetry,* and elsewhere. Wanda is the author of *Rainlily* (2018), *Lady Saturn* (Rhythm & Bones, 2019), *Honey-Laced Garbage Dreams* (Ghost City Press, 2019), and *Venus in Bloom* (Porkbelly Press, 2019).

www.ingramcontent.com/pod-product-compliance
Lightning Source LLC
Chambersburg PA
CBHW060508080526
44584CB00015B/1603